The Lady of Guadalupe

WRITTEN AND ILLUSTRATED BY
Tomie de Paola

Holiday House · New York

for Ethel Souza and Jack Schanhaar

Copyright © 1980 by Tomie de Paola
All rights reserved
Printed in the United States of America

Library of Congress Cataloging in Publication Data

De Paola, Thomas Anthony.
The Lady of Guadalupe.

SUMMARY: Recounts the appearance of the Lady of
Guadalupe to a poor Indian farmer in Mexico in 1531.
1. Guadalupe, Nuestra Señora de—Juvenile literature.
[1. Guadalupe, Nuestra Señora de. 2. Diego,
Juan, fl. 1531] I. Title.
BT660.G8D43   232.91   79-19610
ISBN 0-8234-0373-4
English language paperback edition: ISBN 0-8234-0403-X

Spanish language hard-cover edition: ISBN 0-8234-0374-2
Spanish language paperback edition: ISBN 0-8234-0404-8

Along time ago, in the country now called Mexico, there lived an Indian named Juan Diego.

That was not always his name. Before the white men came across the sea from Spain, Juan Diego was called "He-who-speaks-like-an-eagle." He lived simply in the village of Tolpetlac with his wife, and he planted corn and paid his taxes to the great Aztec Empire.

Some of the white men were called friars. They spoke of one God who was kind and loving like a father.

"He-who-speaks-like-an-eagle" and his wife listened to the friars. They became Christians, and their names were changed to Juan Diego and Maria Lucia. They were faithful to their new religion and had much peace and happiness.

One winter Maria Lucia became ill and died. Juan Diego was heartbroken. But the friars told him not to be sad, that surely a good woman like Maria Lucia was safe in the Kingdom of their new Father.

Juan Diego continued to work hard and, just as he had done when his wife was alive, he went every Saturday to the Church of Santiago to pray at the mass in honor of the Mother of God. And then he would stay for the great celebration of prayers and mass on Sunday.

But one day, on the ninth of December in the year 1531, something happened that would change his life forever.

It was just before dawn that Juan Diego put on his tilma and set out for the Saturday services at the church. It was a fair distance from his village, but Juan Diego was used to it. He traveled on foot at a good pace, as had all his ancestors centuries before him.

When Juan Diego neared the hill of Tepeyac, he heard what he thought was a birdsong. But it was different. It sounded as though a choir of birds was singing the chant that the friars had taught him. It reminded Juan Diego of the music of the High Mass.

Looking up, he saw that the top of the hill was covered by a brilliant white cloud.

He decided to have a closer look.

As Juan Diego got nearer, the cloud seemed to explode in rays of color. And suddenly the music stopped. Silence was all around.

Then Juan Diego heard a human voice—the sweet gentle voice of a woman—speaking in his own language.

"Juan," the voice said. "Juan Diego."

Juan Diego ran to the very top of the hill. As he got there, the cloud parted, and he saw the most beautiful lady dressed in what looked like the robes of an Aztec princess.

Juan Diego threw himself down on his knees. The Lady looked as if she was standing in front of the sun, with light all around her. Everything gleamed and glistened as though made of precious jewels and gold.

"Juan Diego," the Lady said, "smallest and most beloved of my sons . . ."

Juan scrambled to his feet.

"Where are you off to, Juanito?" the Lady asked.

Juan Diego answered as politely as possible, because he could tell he was speaking to a royal person. He told the Lady he was on his way to the Church of Santiago to hear the mass in honor of the Mother of God.

"My very dear son," the Lady said, "I want you to know that I am the Mother of God, and I want you to listen carefully. I have a very important message to give you. I wish to have a church built here, where I can show my love to all your people, the Indians. You must go at once to the house of the Bishop of Mexico and tell him that I have sent you to make this request. Tell him that he must build a church here, right away. Tell him all that you have seen and heard."

Juan Diego was in a daze as he pushed his way through the crowds of the busy city of Mexico. He had no trouble finding the Bishop's house, because all the roads led to the main square. On one side of the square was the Cathedral and the Bishop's home. High white walls and a huge wooden gate surrounded the house.

Juan Diego banged the heavy knocker.

The doorkeeper, an old friar, looked through a peephole and opened a small door in the gate.

"I have important business with His Excellency the Bishop," Juan Diego stammered.

The courtyard was already filled with people, both Indian and Spanish, who had come to ask favors from His Excellency.

Juan Diego went to a corner to wait under a tree. He waited and waited, watching the beggars, clowns, fortune-tellers, and dancers who always showed up where there was a crowd of people.

A friar was walking around questioning those who had come to see the Bishop. He didn't reach Juan Diego until noon.

Juan Diego told the young friar about the Lady and her message but, instead of taking him in to see the Bishop, the friar questioned Juan over and over again.

At last the friar said, "Juan Diego, I'm sure His Excellency will want to hear this from your own lips. But he is a very busy man, so you must be patient and wait until I can arrange an audience for you."

Again Juan Diego waited.

Finally, late in the afternoon, the friar returned and led Juan Diego to a bare room. Sitting on a raised throne sat a small figure in the same brown robes of the friars, surrounded by people. It was the Bishop.

With the help of an interpreter, the Bishop asked, "What is it you wish of us, my son?"

"Only that you build a church for the Mother of God, who spoke to me on the hillside of Tepeyac this morning at dawn and requested me to ask you for this small favor," Juan answered.

Laughter ran through the room. The Bishop raised his hand, and the crowd grew quiet.

Then the Bishop asked Juan all the same questions that the young friar had asked him earlier. Juan told the Bishop everything that had happened.

"My son," the Bishop said slowly in the Aztec language, without the help of an interpreter, "I have many pressing matters of state that I must attend to first. If you will return in a few days and repeat all the details you have so carefully told us, we will think about it. Be patient with us," the Bishop added.

Juan Diego was led out into the courtyard and through the gate.

He had failed. It had never occurred to him that the Lady's request would not be granted.

Juan was tired and sad when he trudged back up the hill of Tepeyac to tell the Lady of his failure.

The Lady was waiting in the same spot.

"Oh, beautiful Lady," Juan Diego sobbed, "I have failed!"

He told her of his visit.

"I'm sure the Bishop did not believe me," Juan continued. "But he did tell me to return in a few days. And he did say he would think seriously about it."

Juan kept apologizing for his failure, saying that perhaps if the Lady sent a child or a noble rather than a poor ignorant farmer . . .

He bowed his head in silence.

"My beloved son," the Lady said, "I have many messengers I could send, but it is you I need and want for this purpose. I beg you to do it for my sake. Go home now to your village. But tomorrow go back to the Bishop and tell him that I demand he build a church here in this very place."

Juan Diego realized that he must do as the Lady asked.

"I will do it," Juan said. "Please, wait for me here tomorrow at the setting of the sun, and I know I will bring you back good news from the Bishop. I leave you in peace now, Lady. God keep you."

The next morning, it was Sunday, the tenth of December. Juan Diego was up before daybreak. This time he reached the Church of Santiago and, after the services, instead of talking with his friends, he set off once more for the Bishop's house.

Again he knocked at the gate, again the doorkeeper let him into the courtyard. And again he waited and waited to see the Bishop.

This time, however, he was led to the Bishop's private study.

Almost as soon as Juan entered the room, the Bishop said severely, "Why have you come back so soon? Didn't I tell you that I needed several days to think about this matter?"

The Bishop questioned Juan Diego again. He was impressed with Juan's sincere answers, and Juan began to think he had won the Bishop over to the Lady's wishes.

But the interpreter said, "His Excellency says that he cannot do what has been asked of him. Juan Diego should go back to this lady and tell her to give him some sort of sign— a sign to make it clear that she is indeed the Mother of God, and it is truly her wish that a church be built!"

"Of course, Your Lordship," Juan Diego answered. "You have only to choose the sign you want, and I'm sure the Lady will be happy to provide it for you."

There was a great deal of whispering, and finally the Bishop told Juan that it was not his place to demand, but that he would be happy with any sort of sign the Lady chose to send him.

After Juan left, the Bishop called two of his most trusted servants and told them to follow Juan Diego and not to let him out of their sight.

Juan went through the gate filled with joy. He hurried to tell the Lady what had happened.

The two servants were Indians and once could run as swiftly and easily as Juan Diego. But now they had grown fat from easy living, so they could not keep up with him.

Juan Diego disappeared completely from sight after he crossed a small bridge over a stream.

The two servants looked everywhere. They crawled under the bridge and got muddy. They followed the stream around the hill. They ran back and forth but Juan Diego seemed to have vanished into thin air.

The servants returned to the Bishop. "This Juan Diego is a wizard-half-tiger with the wings of an eagle," said one of the servants. "He has disappeared."

"He must come from the Devil," said the other.

"We'll take care of him if he comes back," they said, angrily.

But the Bishop was deep in thought and prayer trying to understand this Indian, Juan Diego, with his strange story of the Lady and her message.

Juan Diego had no idea he had been followed. He had returned to the Lady on Tepeyac and told her once more all that had happened.

She smiled at Juan Diego and thanked him for being so patient. She told him to return the next morning, and she would be waiting. Then she would give the good Bishop a sign.

Juan Diego hurried home, happy that soon the Lady's wishes would be granted.

All his neighbors were waiting for him.

"Juan, Juan," they cried. "Juan Bernardino, your uncle, is ill. We are afraid he is dying."

Juan loved his uncle like a father. Juan Bernardino was his only relative still alive, so he rushed to his bedside.

His uncle was indeed ill. He moaned and tossed and had a high fever.

All night, Juan Diego sat and tried to help his uncle with ancient remedies that the wise old women of the village told him about.

He stroked his uncle's sweating body with a feather and a fresh egg, which was then broken and buried in the earth.

Tea made out of herbs and eucalyptus leaves was forced down the old man's throat.

The women wound their long scarves around the poor man and pulled, hoping to squeeze out the fever.

But it was clear to Juan Diego that none of these remedies could save his uncle. In the light before dawn, Juan Diego ran off toward the Church of Santiago to fetch the priest, so his uncle could be given the Last Blessings.

The worry about his uncle caused Juan Diego to completely forget about meeting the Lady. It was only as he approached the hill of Tepeyac that he remembered.

Quickly, he decided that he must get the priest first, then he would keep his promise and go to the Lady. Surely she would understand.

Juan Diego took the path through a gulley at the bottom of the hill. If the Lady was waiting, she would not see him. Just as he came around a jagged section of rock, he saw her!

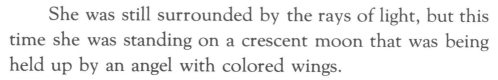

She was still surrounded by the rays of light, but this time she was standing on a crescent moon that was being held up by an angel with colored wings.

And she was descending the hill to meet him.

Juan Diego fell on the ground and covered his head with his tilma.

But the Lady's voice was gentle.

"Where are you going, my little son?" she asked.

Juan Diego sobbed. "Do not be angry," he said, and he told the Lady about his uncle and how he was on his way to fetch the priest.

The Lady listened, and then she spoke again.

"Do you believe that I would neglect someone I love so much, especially when you are doing so much for me? Do not be concerned for your uncle. He will not die of this fever. In fact, he is already cured."

Juan believed the Lady with his whole heart and asked her for the sign she had promised so he could quickly go to the Bishop.

"My dear son," the Lady said, "climb up to the top of the hill where we first met. Cut and gather the roses you will find there. Collect them together in your tilma and bring them here to me. I will tell you what you have to do and say."

Even though Juan knew that no roses grew on that hillside, especially in winter, he ran to the top. And there was the most beautiful garden he had ever seen. Roses of Castile with dew still on their petals stretched as far as he could see.

He cut the best blooms carefully with his stone knife, filled his tilma with them, and hurried back to where the Lady was waiting.

The Lady took the roses, rearranged them, and placed them back in Juan's tilma. Then, tying it around his neck, she told him, "This is the sign that the Bishop wants. Go quickly, and do not stop along the way. Above all, do not show what you are carrying to anyone except the Bishop. When he sees this sign, he will build the church I have asked for."

For the third time, Juan Diego set off to see the Bishop. Only this time, he did not run but walked as swiftly as he could, being careful not to spill the miraculous roses.

Again he was kept waiting at the Bishop's house. And although he was asked what he carried, he refused to show anyone.

The hour grew very late. Poor Juan Diego was beginning to think he would never see the Bishop. And to make matters worse, the two servants who had followed him the night before began to insist that he show them what he carried.

Juan forgot his promise to the Lady and opened his tilma a tiny bit so the two men could glimpse the roses.

But each time the men tried to grab the roses of Castile, they seemed to disappear into the cloth of Juan's tilma.

Frightened, they ran to the Bishop.

They stammered and talked at the same time. "We kept him waiting, hoping he would show us what was in his tilma. We know how busy Your Excellency is. Then we saw that his tilma was full of flowers, not just flowers but roses, roses of Castile, now, in winter. They look freshly cut, with dew on them. . ."

"And then?" said the Bishop.

"Each time we tried to touch them—the roses—it was as if they were painted or woven right into the material of Juan Diego's tilma."

The Bishop grew pale. "Bring Juan Diego to me at once!"

Juan Diego was rushed to the Bishop's study.

Juan spoke. "I have the sign you asked for."

And he opened his tilma and let the roses cascade onto the carpet.

A cry came out of the Bishop's mouth as Juan Diego stood holding open the empty tilma, which was still tied around his neck.

The Bishop and everyone else in the room fell to their knees. And the Bishop began to say the prayer "Hail Mary, full of grace."

Juan answered the prayer with the others. Suddenly he realized that no one was looking at the beautiful roses on the carpet. They were all looking at his tilma.

Juan Diego looked down. His rough cactus-fiber tilma had been changed into a painting of the Lady just as he had last seen her at the foot of Tepeyac.

"Forgive me, my dear son, for my doubts," the Bishop said, as he helped Juan Diego untie the tilma. Quickly a procession was formed, with the Bishop holding the miraculous painting, out through the courtyard still filled with people, into the Bishop's private chapel. The Bishop placed the painting over the altar.

After this ceremony, the Bishop had a long, long conversation alone with Juan Diego. He carefully wrote everything down, especially all the details about the exact spot where the Lady wanted the church built.

Then the Bishop sent a large company of people with Juan Diego, to see if his uncle had indeed been cured.

Sure enough, Juan Bernardino was waiting, surrounded by all the villagers.

And he had great news himself. He told how just as he was at the point of death, a beautiful lady appeared to him, the very Lady who had met with Juan Diego and whose portrait was now on the tilma.

Juan Bernardino also had a message. "The Lady said a church was to be built on the exact spot where she met Juan Diego. She said that it was her wish that the Holy Image should be known as *Our Lady Mary of Guadalupe.*"

When Juan Diego and his uncle returned to the Bishop's house, they found the square filled with thousands of Indians who had heard of the miracle. They came, they said, to see and honor the image of the Lady who wanted to show love to all the people of the New World, but especially to the Indians.

In the space of a few days, an adobe chapel was built at the foot of Tepeyac. The miraculous painting was placed there, and a hut was built for Juan Diego next to it. Juan spent the rest of his life taking care of the shrine.

Eventually, although it was many years later, a great church was built and, to this very day, millions and millions of people come to see the image and pray to the Lady of Guadalupe.

And to this day, the Mexican Indians say to newborn children, "May God be as good to you as he was to Juan Diego."

AUTHOR'S NOTE

Juan Diego's tilma was made of *ayate*, a coarse fabric woven from cactus fiber. Even though it is over 400 years old, it still shows no signs of deterioration. *Ayate* usually deteriorates in ten years or so.

The coloring and technique of the portrait remain mysteries. Over the years, artists have tried, unsuccessfully, to reproduce the unlikely combination of oil, watercolor, tempera, and fresco. The colors have never faded.

Experts disagree on the meaning of the word Guadalupe. Some say it is an Arabic word meaning "hidden river."

Our Lady of Guadalupe is the patron saint of Mexico.

This book was set in Goudy Old Style by Hallmark Press, Inc.
It was printed by offset on 80-lb. Mountie Matte by Rae Publishing Co.

The drawings were done in pencil, inks, and watercolor
on Fabriano 140-lb. hand-made watercolor paper.
Color separations were made by Capper, Inc.